DATE DUE		

Garden of the Spirit Bear

Garden *of the* Spirit Bear

LIFE IN THE GREAT NORTHERN RAINFOREST

by Dorothy Hinshaw Patent
illustrated by Deborah Milton

CLARION BOOKS/NEW YORK

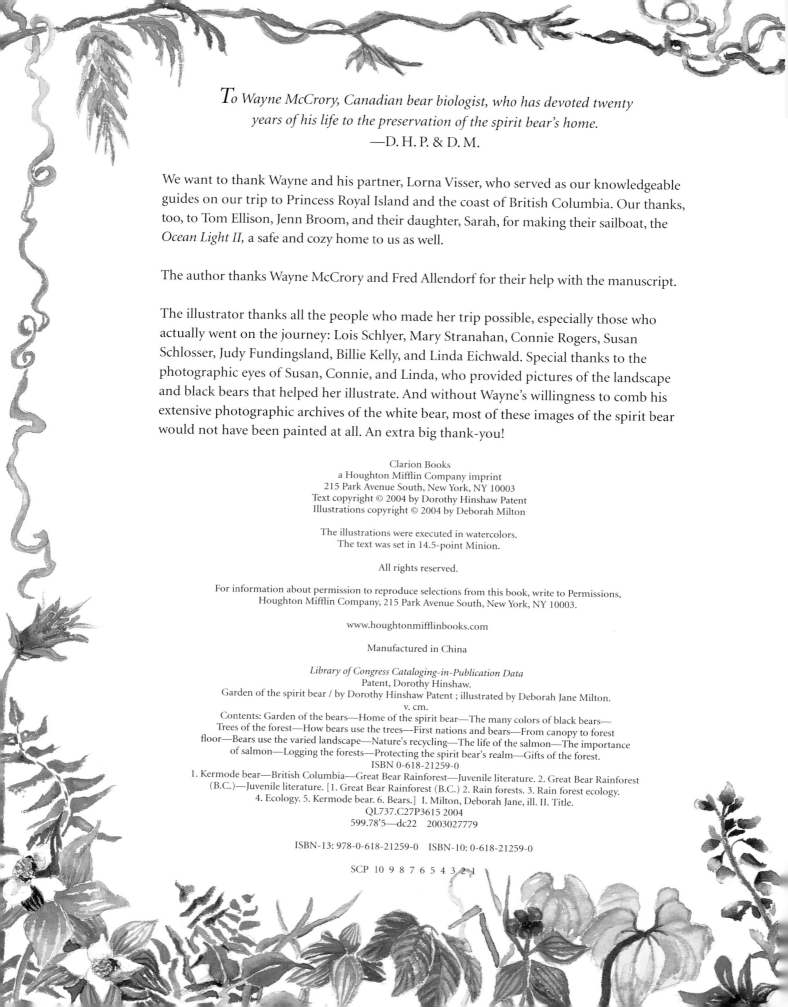

To Wayne McCrory, Canadian bear biologist, who has devoted twenty years of his life to the preservation of the spirit bear's home.
—D. H. P. & D. M.

We want to thank Wayne and his partner, Lorna Visser, who served as our knowledgeable guides on our trip to Princess Royal Island and the coast of British Columbia. Our thanks, too, to Tom Ellison, Jenn Broom, and their daughter, Sarah, for making their sailboat, the *Ocean Light II,* a safe and cozy home to us as well.

The author thanks Wayne McCrory and Fred Allendorf for their help with the manuscript.

The illustrator thanks all the people who made her trip possible, especially those who actually went on the journey: Lois Schlyer, Mary Stranahan, Connie Rogers, Susan Schlosser, Judy Fundingsland, Billie Kelly, and Linda Eichwald. Special thanks to the photographic eyes of Susan, Connie, and Linda, who provided pictures of the landscape and black bears that helped her illustrate. And without Wayne's willingness to comb his extensive photographic archives of the white bear, most of these images of the spirit bear would not have been painted at all. An extra big thank-you!

Clarion Books
a Houghton Mifflin Company imprint
215 Park Avenue South, New York, NY 10003
Text copyright © 2004 by Dorothy Hinshaw Patent
Illustrations copyright © 2004 by Deborah Milton

The illustrations were executed in watercolors.
The text was set in 14.5-point Minion.

www.houghtonmifflinbooks.com

Manufactured in China

Library of Congress Cataloging-in-Publication Data
Patent, Dorothy Hinshaw.
Garden of the spirit bear / by Dorothy Hinshaw Patent ; illustrated by Deborah Jane Milton.
v. cm.
Contents: Garden of the bears—Home of the spirit bear—The many colors of black bears—Trees of the forest—How bears use the trees—First nations and bears—From canopy to forest floor—Bears use the varied landscape—Nature's recycling—The life of the salmon—The importance of salmon—Logging the forests—Protecting the spirit bear's realm—Gifts of the forest.
ISBN 0-618-21259-0
1. Kermode bear—British Columbia—Great Bear Rainforest—Juvenile literature. 2. Great Bear Rainforest (B.C.)—Juvenile literature. [1. Great Bear Rainforest (B.C.) 2. Rain forests. 3. Rain forest ecology. 4. Ecology. 5. Kermode bear. 6. Bears.] I. Milton, Deborah Jane, ill. II. Title.
QL737.C27P3615 2004
599.78'5—dc22   2003027779

ISBN-13: 978-0-618-21259-0   ISBN-10: 0-618-21259-0

SCP 10 9 8 7 6 5 4 3 2 1

Contents

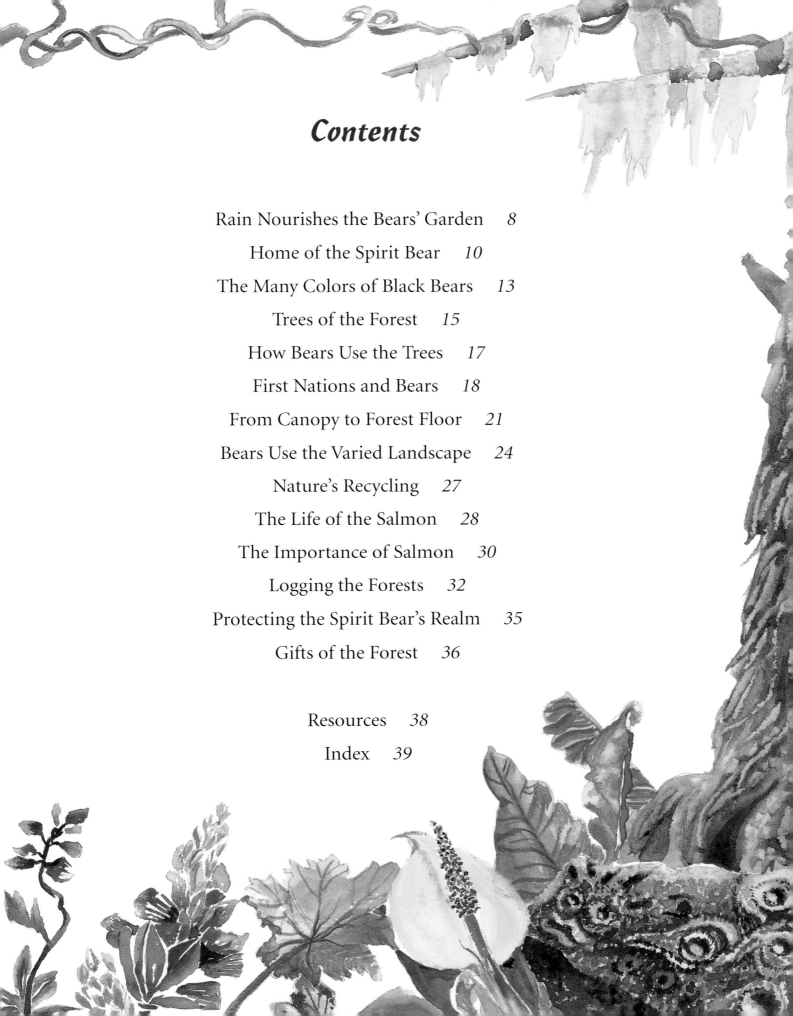

Rain Nourishes the Bears' Garden   8

Home of the Spirit Bear   10

The Many Colors of Black Bears   13

Trees of the Forest   15

How Bears Use the Trees   17

First Nations and Bears   18

From Canopy to Forest Floor   21

Bears Use the Varied Landscape   24

Nature's Recycling   27

The Life of the Salmon   28

The Importance of Salmon   30

Logging the Forests   32

Protecting the Spirit Bear's Realm   35

Gifts of the Forest   36

Resources   38

Index   39

Queen
Charlotte
Islands

PROPOSED SPIRIT BEAR PRESERVE —→
Area of detail

BRITISH COLUMBIA
(CANADA)

Vancouver
Island

Pacific Ocean

Vancouver

Victoria

WASHINGTON
(USA)

Seattle

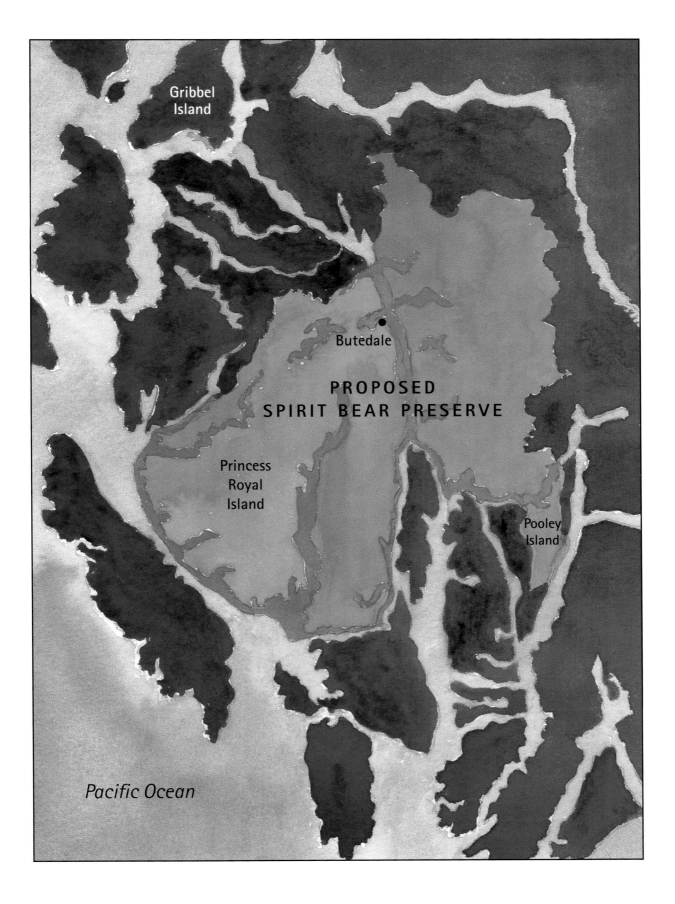

Gribbel
Island

Butedale

PROPOSED
SPIRIT BEAR PRESERVE

Princess
Royal
Island

Pooley
Island

Pacific Ocean

Rain Nourishes the Bears' Garden

Far to the north along the Pacific coast lies the garden of the bears. Here abundant rainfall nourishes everything from bright green grasses and colorful wildflowers to ancient, towering cedar and spruce trees, providing a perfect habitat for bears and other wildlife. Old-growth rainforest like this, with trees up to a thousand or more years old, once extended from northern California into Alaska.

This area is so rainy because of a current of warm seawater that begins near Japan and flows across the Pacific Ocean all the way to North America. It brings warm air and waterlogged clouds with it. When they reach the coast, the clouds release rain, rain, and more rain. Fall and winter storms can spread up and down the coast for hundreds of miles and can last for days. Each year, up to 500 centimeters (about 200 inches) of rain falls.

The southernmost of these rainforests are now mostly gone, felled by the axes and big saws of settlers and loggers. The once-abundant wildlife has also disappeared or become rare, because without trees, the animals and other forest plants cannot survive.

Luckily, much of the ancient forest still remains in Canada and Alaska. Logging companies, however, value the magnificent trees only for their timber, and they have plans for clear-cutting. If they succeed, this bountiful and important environment could become a thing of the past.

Home of the Spirit Bear

The rainforest along the British Columbia coast is a region of deep forests and open meadows, rugged coastal fjords and magical islands. Named the Great Bear Rainforest, it is home to many grizzlies as well as a unique type of black bear called the spirit bear. The chances of viewing this mysterious, rarely seen animal are greatest on Princess Royal, Gribbel, and Pooley Islands. Most spirit bears are black, but one in ten is pure or creamy white, often with a mantle of golden fur across its shoulders. These special animals do not have the pink eyes and noses of albinos (animals that lack the dark pigment called melanin). Instead, their noses are dark and their eyes are brown. Altogether, there are fewer than 150 of these rare and beautiful white bears alive today.

The native people, who call themselves the First Nations, have a story to explain the white bears. According to this legend, Raven, who created the world, visited the land while it was warming and greening up after the chill of the last Ice Age. He chose one special area of the Great Bear Rainforest around Princess Royal Island. There he made every tenth bear white, so that the people would always remember that the land had once been covered with ice and snow.

The Many Colors of Black Bears

Scientists also have something to say about spirit bears, which they consider a subspecies of the American black bear. Black bears inhabit forests across North America, from Alaska to Mexico and from the Pacific coast to the Atlantic. Females weigh up to 140 kilograms (about 300 pounds), whereas males can be twice as heavy and can be 90 centimeters (almost 3 feet) tall at the shoulder. The bears live a solitary life, except during the mating season in early summer and while the female is raising her cubs.

The name "black bear" is confusing, because these animals actually come in many colors. In the northeastern United States most of them are black, but in other areas brown, cinnamon, and even silvery gray-blue ones are found. Only the spirit bear, which lives along the Canadian coast, is sometimes white. A black spirit bear can have white cubs, and a white one can have black cubs. While some people use the name "spirit bear" exclusively for white individuals, scientists call all of them—black and white alike—spirit bears. Their other name is the Kermode (ker-MODE-ee) bear, after Francis Kermode, a museum curator who took an interest in them early in the twentieth century.

Trees of the Forest

For thousands of years, both bears and people have depended on the great trees of the forest, especially the magnificent red cedar and its cousin, the yellow cedar. A red cedar can grow to 70 meters (230 feet) in height, and the base of its trunk can be 4.3 meters (14 feet) in diameter. Yellow cedar is smaller and less common.

Other long-lived trees also dominate the coastal rainforest. Like the cedars, they are conifers, trees that bear their seeds within cones and have small, pointed leaves called needles. Conifers are well adapted to life along the Pacific coast. There is abundant rain during the fall and winter, although summers can be dry. Conifers survive the dry spells, because their needles don't lose water as easily as the broad, thin leaves of trees like maples and elms. The needles are also able to gather moisture from the fog that often envelops the forest during the summer and fall.

Three kinds of conifers other than cedars are especially common in the Great Bear Rainforest. The magnificent Douglas fir is the second tallest tree in the world, occasionally reaching almost 90 meters (300 feet) tall and living more than a thousand years. The shade-tolerant western hemlock grows slowly and occasionally lives more than 500 years. The world's fourth tallest tree, the Sitka spruce, dwells within 50 kilometers (about 30 miles) of the seacoast. It can grow to well over 60 meters (about 200 feet).

How Bears Use the Trees

Kermode bears couldn't survive without these old trees. They use the hollow trunks of ancient trees as protected dens, where they spend the winter in a sleeplike state called hibernation. Their tiny cubs are born during this time. Usually, two or three cubs make up a litter, but there can be as many as five. When born, each weighs less than 330 grams (12 ounces), no more than a can of soda pop.

The cubs grow fast, however, fed by their mother's rich milk. By the time they leave the den in the spring, they weigh from 2.25 to 4.5 kilograms (5 to 10 pounds), the size of a small dog. They can now use trees for safety, clambering up them to avoid danger.

The cubs' mother protects them and teaches them what foods are good to eat. From her they learn how to fish. By the time they are six to eight months old, they no longer need their mother's milk. But they stay with her through the next winter, denning together once again in the hollow trunk of a great tree.

First Nations and Bears

Before the arrival of European Americans, the First Nations people also used the great trees for their homes. Seaside villages of massive cedar longhouses were marked by giant cedar totem poles. The poles were carved with images of animals identifying the different tribal clans, such as eagles, killer whales, wolves, ravens, and, of course, bears.

Bears have always been especially respected by native peoples. Many ancient stories feature them. Sometimes, a human is transformed into a bear, or a bear turns out to be a human in disguise. In one such story from the Tsimshian (TSIM-shee-an), a group of First Nations people who share the Great Bear Rainforest with the spirit bear, a famous hunter pursues a white bear up a steep mountain and across two gorges that the bear creates by kicking at the mountain. The bear climbs a ladder to the sky, and the hunter follows. There a path leads through a beautiful prairie to a house, which the bear enters. When the hunter peeks through a hole in the wall, he sees a young woman removing the bear skin she has been wearing as a disguise. She shakes out the ashes that made it look white. Then the hunter is ushered into the house and is married to the girl, who turns out to be the daughter of a great chief.

From Canopy to Forest Floor

The old-growth coastal rainforest is the home of many living things besides trees, bears, and people. Soft green moss envelopes the tree branches. Ferns perch high among the mosses, decorating the branches with their frilly fronds. Mats and strands of ancient lichens, with names like old-man's-beard, decorate the trunks and hang from the branches.

The uppermost layer of the rainforest, called the canopy, shades the rest of the forest. The canopy is made up of the tops and branches of the tallest trees. Birds such as bald eagles nest there. Even a small seabird called the marbled murrelet uses the mossy branches of huge old trees to nest in and rear its young. Closer to the ground, along the trunks and lower branches, live other animals, such as bats, which pass the days sleeping in deep grooves in the tree bark.

The moist forest floor, covered by moss and rotting leaves, is home to shade-loving plants such as twinflowers and deer ferns. Shrubs like devil's-club, wild currants, and red huckleberries grow beneath the great trees, especially near the river banks, where light can peek through. Dark-eyed juncos hop about, looking for food, while grouse wander along the forest trails made by bears and other large animals as they search for food and water. On the forest floor, giant banana slugs up to 10 centimeters (4 inches) long feed on food such as dead leaves.

Altogether, 68 kinds of mammals, from tiny mice to giant bears, live here, as well as 230 bird species. Countless kinds of insects and other small creatures also live in the ground, on the forest floor, and in the trees.

Bears Use the Varied Landscape

Although we call this region a rainforest, much of the land isn't blanketed by trees. Ice- and snow-covered mountains mark the inland edges of the area, and the landscape is dotted with bogs and ponds, where bears can wallow. Along the lower stretches of the rivers lie estuaries, where coastal tides flood the land. Trees don't grow well here. Instead, dense fields of grass and grasslike sedges cover the ground, interspersed with chocolate lilies, sweet angelica, and other wildflowers. Only the grizzly bears have claws and shoulder muscles powerful enough to dig up the roots and bulbs of these plants, but spirit bears relish the sedges and grasses. They also eat the berries and crab apples that grow along the estuaries and the edges of the forest. Both bear species have a diet similar to our own—a wide mix of animal and vegetable foods, including leafy plants, roots, fruit, insects, mice, and salmon. Bears also use plants as medicine, and native peoples have learned about healing plants by noticing what plants bears eat when they are sick.

Nature's Recycling

In the Great Bear Rainforest, everything depends on everything else in an endless cycle of renewal. When a dead tree falls, moss and lichen soon cover it. Gradually, insects, fungi, and bacteria eat away at it, softening the wood. Tree seeds land on the log. The moist, moss-covered rotting log provides a perfect nursery for them. Seeds can survive and sprout there, and the gap in the canopy created by the fallen tree allows vital sunlight through. Straight rows of young trees stretch through the forest, showing where the bodies of once great giants fell.

The heavy rainfall enables abundant growth, but plants also need nutrients, such as nitrogen, phosphorus, and potassium. They get some of these with the help of fungi. A mushroom that pokes its way through the ground is only a tiny part of a fungus. Under the ground lies a vast network of microscopically thin strands of fungus connected to the mushroom. The soil of the old-growth forest floor is home to almost two tons of these tiny threads per acre! The strands connect with the roots of the trees and other plants, trading nutrients that they gather for sugars made by green plants such as trees. During the summer, when rain is less abundant, the fungi also help the trees absorb water.

The Life of the Salmon

Salmon are the key to the rainforest's health. Adult salmon spawn, or lay their eggs, in the rivers and streams. The young salmon swim down the rivers into the ocean. They live there for years, returning only when fully grown and ready to spawn. The biggest species, the chinook, can reach over 55 kilograms (125 pounds). As they grow, the salmon incorporate nutrients from the sea into their bodies. When they swim back to the streams and rivers where they were born, they bring these vital chemicals with them.

As a male salmon reaches maturity, his colors become more intense, and his lower jaw develops a prominent hook. Males and females alike must struggle against the current of the rivers, swollen by fall rains. The fish remember the smell of their home streams and follow that scent as they jump through the rapids and swim along the sides of the river to avoid the fastest current. This makes them easy prey for bears, which may catch and eat a half-dozen fish in an hour.

When they arrive at the spawning beds, the female salmon clear away nests, called redds, in the gravel. The male and female swim next to each other as the female releases her eggs and the male his sperm, which fertilize the eggs. The nest is covered with gravel and a new one is made. The pair may spawn off and on over a number of days. Finally, spent and exhausted, the fish become weaker and weaker and eventually die.

The Importance of Salmon

An adult Kermode bear preparing for winter hibernation fattens up by eating as many salmon as it can catch. It may also eat the dead, spawned-out salmon. Some of the nutrients in the salmon are deposited on the forest floor when they leave the bear's body through its urine and feces. Small bears sometimes drag dead salmon into the forest to feed, undisturbed by big bears, and leave some uneaten. When these remains decay, nutrients are released into the ground. And when the bears, wolves, and other animals that eat the salmon die, their bodies also decay, returning more nutrients to the system.

The nutrients from salmon allow the trees to grow big and tall. In turn, the trees protect the streams that the salmon need for breeding. Fallen logs in streams help break up the downward rush of water, creating gravel beds for spawning salmon and quiet pools where the young fish can thrive. When heavy rain pounds the forest, tree branches break the fall of the drops, spreading out the time it takes for water to reach the forest floor. In the old-growth forest, stream levels rise gradually after a storm. But in the younger, less healthy forests that grow back after logging, stream levels rise much faster, and the strong current can wash away the salmon eggs.

Logging the Forests

In modern times, life has become difficult for salmon. Many of the rivers that they must navigate have been dammed, and once-great salmon runs have died out or been heavily reduced. The salmon that spawn in rivers and streams in the Great Bear Rainforest are doing well, but that could quickly be changed by logging.

Logging once consisted of choosing the particular trees you wanted and cutting only them. But during the twentieth century, giant machines that could easily mow down entire forests changed logging completely. Now logging almost always means clear-cutting—cutting down every single tree. Only the trees that are wanted are taken. Left behind are piles of unwanted timber and brush to be burned.

After clear-cutting, there are no more trees to shade the ground and water, no more hollow trees where bears can den. Water evaporates from streams, drying up and killing salmon eggs. The water heats up, making it too warm for young salmon. On the land, weeds and scrub replace the forests, and wildlife, including bears, disappears. A beautiful green forest full of life becomes an ugly, scarred wasteland.

An area that has been logged may be replanted with fast-growing trees that, when grown, are also clear-cut. The old-growth forest doesn't get a chance to regrow, and the logging roads bring in more human disturbance, including hunters, some of whom illegally kill bears, deer, and wolves.

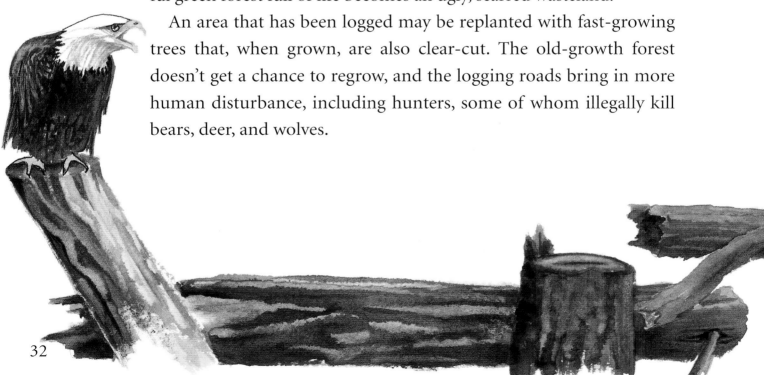

Protecting the Spirit Bear's Realm

During the 1980s, as logging companies planned their future clear-cuts, an organization called the Valhalla Wilderness Society studied the central coast of British Columbia to find out what areas needed to be protected in order to save the spirit bear and its realm. Logging companies had already destroyed some of its precious, limited habitat.

Using the information it gathered, along with input from First Nations people, the Valhalla Wilderness Society proposed the Spirit Bear Conservancy, a protected area where logging and other development would be prohibited. First Nations people would still be able to use the area in traditional ways.

The proposed sanctuary would protect the core of the spirit bear's realm, which is home to between 800 and 1,200 Kermode bears. It takes at least 500 individuals of a species to maintain a healthy population, so this number isn't very large. The sanctuary lies about midway between the cities of Vancouver and Prince Rupert and includes the southern two-thirds of Princess Royal Island, part of Pooley Island, and areas on the mainland that would link the sanctuary to other protected landscapes further inland.

The Spirit Bear Conservancy would also protect the spawning grounds of salmon—an estimated population of 160,000 fish. Thousands of Sitka black-tailed deer; dozens of gray wolves and grizzly bears; rare and endangered species such as the marbled murrelet, tailed frog, pine marten, and wolverine; and endangered salt marshes, estuaries, and forest types—all would be given the opportunity to thrive.

Gifts of the Forest

In 2001, the government of British Columbia agreed that the spirit bear and its land deserved protection and announced the Spirit Bear Protection Area. However, the government decided to protect only about half of what the Valhalla Wilderness Society had proposed. The society continues to work toward protecting more land.

All living things, including human beings, ultimately require intact ecosystems for survival. If enough land is set aside to protect the spirit bear, people as well as nature will benefit. The trees of the forest remove carbon dioxide from the air, helping to slow global warming. They also help maintain the normal climate system of North America. The coastal rainforests yield salmon for us to eat, and careful, selective logging outside the sanctuary could provide construction material for our homes. The Spirit Bear Conservancy would be a living museum, where people for generations to come could visit and be reminded how the earth used to be. The more we can save of this beautiful ecosystem, the healthier our planet will be now and in the future.

Resources

Three books with lots of color photographs give information about the Pacific coastal rainforest: *America's Rainforest,* by Gerry Ellis and Karen Kane (Minocqua, Wis.: NorthWord Press, 1991) describes the coastal forest from California to Alaska. In *The Great Bear Rainforest: Canada's Forgotten Coast,* Ian and Karen McAllister, with Cameron Young (San Francisco: Sierra Club Books, 1997), describe their travels by boat along the Canadian coast, informing the reader about the rainforest in the process. Charles Russell's unique experiences with one friendly wild white bear are described and illustrated in *Spirit Bear: Encounters with the White Bear of the Western Rainforest* (Toronto: Key Porter Books Limited, 1994).

Two organizations work hard to preserve the Great Bear Rainforest: The Valhalla Wilderness Society, Box 329, New Denver, British Columbia, Canada VOG 1S0 (www.savespiritbear.org), has spearheaded the effort to save the spirit bear and its rainforest home.

The Raincoast Conservation Society, P.O. Box 8663, Victoria, British Columbia, Canada V8W 3S2 (www.raincoast.org), sponsors studies such as a recent one on the unique gray wolves of the forest, as well as works to protect and restore rainforest ecosystems.

In Alaska, much of the rainforest still remains, but logging companies are pressuring to log as much as possible. For more information about the Tongass National Forest, which at 16.8 million acres is the single largest national forest in America, contact:

Forest Service Information Center
Centennial Hall
101 Eagan Drive
Juneau, AK 99801

(http://www.vacationalaska.com/info/publiclands/tongas.html)

Index

Note: Page numbers in **bold** type refer to illustrations.

albinos, 10
animals:
   carved images of, 18, **18, 19**
   in rainforests, 21–22, **23,** 24
   and recycling nutrients, 30–31
   survival of, 9, 17, 32, 35

banana slugs, 22
bats, 21
bears, **11, 13, 22, 27**
   colors of, 10, **12,** 13
   food for, 24, **24, 25,** 30, **30**
   hibernation of, 17
   Kermode (spirit), 13
   legends of, 10, 18
   protecting the habitat of, 35
   in rainforest, 10, 24
   range of, 13
   and salmon, 29, 30, 30
   sizes of, 13, 17
   teaching survival skills, 17
   trees used by, **16,** 17
birds, 21, 22

canopy, 21
cedar trees, 15
chinook salmon, 28
clear-cutting, 9, 32, **33**
conifers, 15
cubs, 13, **13**
   birth of, 17
   dens for, **16,** 17
   learning from mother bear, 17
   sizes of, 17

diet, 24
Douglas fir, 15

eagles, **14,** 21
ecosystems, 36

ferns, 21, 22
First Nations:
   legends of, 10, 18
   plants as medicine for, 24
   protecting the forest, 35
   totem poles of, 18, **19**
   and trees, 18
fish, *see* salmon
flowers, 8, 22, 24
forests, *see* rainforests
fungi (mushrooms), 27, **27**

grasses, 8, 24
Great Bear Rainforest, **20, 26**
   legends of, 10, 18
   recycling in, 27, **27,** 30–31
   streams of, 31, 32
   threat of logging in, 32, **33**
   trees of, 15, 31
Gribbel Island, **7,** 10
grizzly bears, 10, 24, 35

hemlock, western, 15
hibernation, 17
hunters, 32

Kermode, Francis, 13
Kermode bear (spirit bear), 13

lichens, 21, **26,** 27, **27**
logging, 9, **33**
 clear-cutting, 32
 and streams, 31, 32
 as threat to nature, 32

marbled murrelet, 21, **30,** 35
medicine, plants as, 24
melanin, 10
mice, 22, **23**
moss, 21, 22, 27, **27**
mushrooms, 27, **27**

nitrogen, 27
nutrients, 27, 28, 30–31

phosphorus, 27
plants:
 as food, 24
 as medicine, 24
 nutrients for, 27
potassium, 27
Pooley Island, **7,** 10
Princess Royal Island:
 legend of, 10
 protection of, 35

rain, 8
rainforests, 8–9, **20, 26**
 animals and plants in, 21–22,
  23, 24
 bears at home in, 10, 24
 canopy of, 21
 clear-cutting of, 9, 32, **33**
 landscape of, 24

rainforests (*cont.*)
 protection of, 35
 recycling in, 27, **27,** 30–31
 and salmon, 28
 streams in, 31, 32
 trees of, *see* trees
Raven, legend of, 10
recycling, in nature, 27, **27,** 30–31
redds (salmon nests), 29

salmon, 28–31, **28, 29,** 32
 protecting the habitat of, 35
 spawning, 29, 31, 35
sedges, 24
seeds, of trees, 27
Sitka spruce, 15
spawning, 29, 31, 35
spider web, **21**
spirit bear, *see* bears
Spirit Bear Conservancy, 35, 36

totem poles, 18, **19**
trees, 8, **14,** 15
 and air quality, 36
 and animal survival, 9, 35
 and First Nations, 18
 logging of, 9, 32, **33**
 recycling with, 27, **27,** 31
 seeds of, 27
 totem poles made from, 18, **19**
 used by bears, **16,** 17
Tsimshian people, 18

Valhalla Wilderness Society, 35, 36
Vancouver, 6